HOW

TO

OVERCOME

REJECTION

The Ultimate Strategies to Deal with Rejection, Heal from Regret and Shame, Build Your Self-Worth for a Better Tomorrow

Charity Belle, PhD.

TABLE OF CONTENTS

INTRODUCTION

Have you just been rejected? Or did you just reject somebody else? Rejection occurs frequently, and it is awful. Understanding the causes of rejection and putting some coping mechanisms into practice can be useful if you're having a hard time handling it. We'll cover all of these topics and more in this book.

We all desire and require the ability to feel cherished, accepted, and taken care of. One of the fundamental psychological requirements for human existence, it begins in childhood and lasts all the way through adulthood. Because of this, enduring emotional neglect of any kind or degree and the anxiety associated with it are harsh and unstable. And why does it sting when even a loved one ignores you?

If any of these psychological conditions are causing you mental stress right now, you might want to consider enrolling in a love addiction intensive class where you can learn techniques for reducing, accepting, and overcoming rejection pain. The first step in improving your emotional well-being is to get knowledge about the specifics of emotional rejection and how, if ignored, they can have a detrimental effect on your life.

Pushing someone or anything away can be characterized as rejection. One could be rejected by one's own family, a friend, or a romantic partner, and the ensuing emotions are frequently terrible. In daily life, rejection can be felt in significant or minor ways. Even while rejection is frequently a part of life, some kinds of rejection might be harder to handle than others. An individual may be able to deal with rejection and the associated distress with assistance from a therapist or other mental health specialist.

There are several situations where rejection can happen. Rejection typically refers to a situation in which someone or something is pushed aside or out. For instance, someone might reject or refuse to accept a present. Rejection is most often used in the context of mental health treatment to describe the sentiments of loss, sadness, or guilt that result from not being accepted by others. After a significant other ends a relationship, a person could feel rejected. When a child has few or no friends, they could feel excluded by their peers. An individual who was abandoned for adoption could also feel rejected.

Rejection can also be the outcome of life experiences that have nothing to do with romantic relationships, such being passed over for a job you really wanted or getting a rejection letter from college. Even while rejection hurts, some rejections could be more hurtful than others. Being rejected can generate bad sensations and emotions because the majority of people need social interaction and acceptance from society.

CHAPTER 2
CLASSES OF REJECTION

There are four basic sorts of rejection, each of which comes with its own set of psychological challenges and emotional burdens. No matter what form of rejection you are experiencing, it is always advisable to get assistance if you are finding it difficult to deal with and accept the circumstance. Rejection can occur in a variety of scenarios, and any mental health effects will partly rely on those contexts. Common forms of rejection include:

- **Family Rejection**

This can take the form of abuse, abandonment, neglect, or the withholding of love and affection. Parental rejection is the most common of the family rejection. An individual is likely to be affected by this kind of rejection for the rest of their lives, and it could have negative effects.

Parental rejection is the most frequent form of this kind of rejection, but it can also occur amongst siblings. It may also involve many forms of emotional abuse, as well as neglect, abandonment, and a lack of care and love. People who experience this form of emotional rejection may suffer the effects for the rest of their life.

- **Social Rejection**

This kind of rejection can happen to anyone at any age and frequently starts in early infancy. Bullying and alienation at work or at school are two examples of social rejection, although it can affect any social group. People who live "outside the norm" for their society or who oppose the status quo may be more likely to experience social rejection.

People typically experience this kind of rejection quite early in life. It can include everything ranging from bullying of various types to school exclusion. However, it can affect people of all ages, including adults and members of different social groups. People who tend to challenge the status quo are more vulnerable to this kind of rejection.

Why Does Social Rejection Occur?

Every human has a deep need to fit in. Some argue that this is because humans don't have claws or fangs, making us relatively susceptible to predators; remaining in a group helped us survive. Because of this, those of us who were more focused toward groups survived. As a result, all modern people are very group-oriented.

Whether or not this evolutionary explanation is accurate, we do know that having a feeling of community, social involvement, and relational commitment is important for our health, pleasure, and even survival. The most advantageous factor for our health and wellbeing may actually be social connection. Our sense of belonging consists of two components and they are:

- It entails routinely having constructive social interactions.
- It offers a solid framework based on shared concern.

Being a part of a community not only makes us feel like we belong, but it also validates our essential beliefs and gives us a sense of self-worth. Overall, this makes social approval incredibly essential to us and causes us to feel great anguish when it happens.

- **Relationship Rejection**

People may encounter rejection during courting or in a committed relationship. Examples include withholding affection or closeness from a spouse, refusing to share an experience or occasion with them, or treating them like a passing acquaintance. A person's decision to end a relationship can sometimes make the other partner feel unwelcome.

Romantic connections are typically the only context for this kind of rejection. It might be anything from your partner refusing to share a personal moment with you to the relationship actually ending. This kind of rejection typically results in rapid, severe emotional distress. In these situations, lengthy coaching sessions might be quite helpful.

- **Romantic Rejection**

This can happen when someone requests a date but one is turned down. Although this might sometimes be referred to as sexual rejection, a person who has been rejected romantically might not always be interested in having a sexual connection.

Any sort of rejection can be painful, but when it comes from a trusted loved one, it can have a particularly negative effect on one's sense of self-worth and self-confidence. Therapy can help people heal from wounds that may result from being rejected by a loved one, but it can also help people learn to accept rejection that happens in day-to-day life, such as being rejected by a potential romantic partner, being rejected during a job search, or being rejected when applying to college.

The 'Friend Zone' and Romantic Rejection

Romantic rejection can be extremely difficult, especially for those who want a long-term commitment. When a love relationship ends or you are rejected by a partner, you may experience intense grief that lasts for weeks, months, or even years. Long after a romantic relationship has ended, rejection can change how a person sees their life and themselves.

The idea of the "friend zone" has gained popularity recently. A person who says they were "put in the friend zone" is usually referring to the rejection of amorous advances made on the person they were interested in. Typically, this happens in one of two situations:

- When a person has come to have romantic sentiments for a friend.
- When a person tries to date someone who only wants to pursue friendship with him or her.

Although anyone can use the phrase "being friend zoned" to describe a situation of rejection, the phrase is most frequently used by and by males who have been rejected by women, and is seen by many as problematic.

While many people might be able to accept that the person whom they are attracted to doesn't feel the same way, others could feel furious or disappointed. Some people could think that by being kind to someone, they merit the opportunity to date that person and win their affection. Others might think that maintaining a friendship with someone they are attracted to will offer them the chance to develop romantic feelings for them and the urge to seek a romantic relationship with them.

These concepts have the potential to reinforce the beliefs that romantic love is preferable to friendship, that people (usually men and women) cannot be friends without wanting to have sex, and that everyone wants to have sex (eliminating the experiences of individuals who are aromantic or asexual).

The phrase "man and woman" is not usually used in that sense. When used in this way, it can reinforce the notion that women, or anyone who rejects another, cannot be held accountable for their own attractions or dating preferences and may not know what they want. This implies that when a woman rejects a man, she may not really mean it or may respond differently in the future. The idea that people are heterosexual unless they explicitly indicate differently or that heterosexuality is the "normal" sexual orientation is another reason why the "friend zone" can be said to contribute to heterosexist ideas.

Typically, the term "man and woman" does not have that connotation. The idea that women, or anybody who rejects another, cannot be held responsible for their own attractions or dating choices and might not know what they want can be reinforced when utilized in this manner. This suggests that a woman might not mean it when she rejects a man or that she might act differently in the future. Another way that the "friend zone" can be argued to contribute to heterosexist views is the belief that people are heterosexual unless they expressly state otherwise or that heterosexuality is the "normal" sexual orientation.

CHAPTER 3
FORMATS OF REJECTION

No marriage will always be sunshine and butterflies. Because relationships are complicated, communication problems can arise. Your significant partner and you won't always agree on everything. You have probably encountered some sort of rejection in your marriage at some point. You might experience rejection in many different ways, including both physically and emotionally.

Rejection is inevitable in life, but the manner in which your partner rejects you can reveal a lot about your marriage. Does your partner make concessions or entirely disregard you? Whether or not the relationship is healthy can be determined by how they respond to your "no" and how you decide to handle it.

How exactly should you respond when the person you love rejects you? The most typical sorts of rejection are listed below, along with some tips on how to handle the sensation of being passed over.

- **Silent Rejection**

It can be utterly upsetting when your partner ignores you after you pour your whole heart and soul into your marriage. Because it makes you feel so horrible about yourself, being ignored can be as painful as receiving a flat "no". You may become irritated and angry because you believe your partner doesn't want to be around you. Rejection can be extremely difficult to overcome for people who have poor self-esteem and might cause further setbacks. You and your spouse should have some serious conversations if this type of rejection occurs frequently since it is never appropriate in a marriage. If it is not appropriately addressed, it will cause your marriage to fail.

- **Careless Rejection**

Having your partner tell you "No" outright is the hardest kind of rejection. The last thing you want to do is give your spouse the impression that you are extremely unkind and unpleasant. Because you do receive a response, it's better than being entirely ignored, but that doesn't make it any less painful. Taking a step back from your feelings and evaluating the matter logically is the greatest approach to bounce back from an outright rejection. Why do you believe your partner is acting so hostile? Do you and your partner need to talk about anything else right now in your relationship? It's crucial to attempt to avoid starting a brawl right after this chilly rejection. Instead, calm yourself before attempting to explain why this wounded you.

- **Consensual Rejection**

Sometimes when your partner rejects you, they provide a compromise to try to lessen the impact. Being given the chance to try again in the future makes this kind of rejection the easiest to deal with. It serves as a reminder that your spouse isn't refusing your request out of spite for you; rather, there is a rationale behind it that probably has nothing to do with you. It will depend on your decision how to respond to this kind of rejection how things develop. If you continue to be furious, your spouse may believe that you don't value their feelings or care about the reasons they are rejecting you.

Both you and your partner will have opportunities to improve if you decide to accept the suggested compromise and talk about it civilly.

- **Courteous Rejection**

A rejection, even one that is politely phrased, can seriously affect your performance. No matter how kindly your partner was about the denial, it still causes you to pause and consider your options. It aches! Additionally, this extends beyond your spouse's rejection. According to a University of Michigan Medical School study, the brain responds to social rejection in a manner similar to how it responds to physical harm.

They did observe, however, that the more you become accustomed to receiving polite rejection, the less painful it is to deal with it. You will eventually become more accustomed to rejection as you open up to your spouse, to the point that it no longer negatively affects you. Naturally, this only applies if your partner behaves in a kind, peaceful way.

Your self-esteem can suffer if you are rejected, and it can make you feel unwelcome in your marriage. See if there are any other methods for your spouse to express their sentiments about choosing to say "no" to you without making you feel unwanted. Even if you and your partner don't always have to agree on everything, a lack of regular communication can quickly derail your relationship.

CHAPTER 4
THE PHASES OF REJECTION

How many times can someone be rejected? Understanding rejection is helpful before you can accept your feelings. In terms of emotions, accepting rejection is a process, much like grieving a loss. You will progress through the stages as you work through your emotions, finally getting past the frustration, self-doubt, and anger you are currently feeling to move on and find serenity.

Depending on you and the circumstance, you will spend varying amounts of time dealing with rejection. Some might move more swiftly than others. It's critical to practice self-compassion. There is no ideal rate for overcoming rejection.

The five stages of rejection are listed below:

1. Refusal

Your initial response when learning someone has rejected you will be shock. There must be an error. You might sense that something isn't quite right since you deserve this person's respect and admiration.

2. Anger

That's denial, and after realizing that your rejection wasn't the result of a miscommunication, you'll start to feel upset. You can become enraged once you discover the person rejecting you isn't seeing their error in judgment.

It could be tempting to lash out at the individual who rejected you at this time. Not at all. In the end, yelling at them will just make you feel worse about yourself. Take a few deep breaths and try to relax. You must strive to control your wrath in this case and allow calmer heads prevail.

3. Negotiating

You'll reach a moment where you start to believe that the person who let you down did so due to an incorrect assumption or a lack of knowledge. You'll believe that if you could simply communicate with them, you could influence them.

If you let it, this stage could quickly turn into something frightful for the other person. You must give the person who rejected you some room. For the sake of your potential future relationship, should you both decide to pursue it, you must graciously accept their decision. They are not required to give you a reason for their rejection.

4. Depression

A tangled knot of emotions accompanies rejection. You're sad, ashamed, puzzled, hurt, and angry on top of being disappointed and outraged. Your self-worth may be in question, and your confidence has suffered. These are all legitimate reactions to rejection that may induce depressive symptoms.

You need to put your self-care routine on high alert right now. Make yourself comfortable with friends, light candles, or take a bubble bath. everything that makes you feel cozy. As soon as you feel at ease, start probing your emotions to determine which ones are causing your depression and develop a strategy to deal with them. Reminding yourself of all the reasons you are a fantastic person and of all the people who care about and cherish you could be all that is necessary.

5. Recognition

It's time to analyze the circumstance now that your emotions have stabilized and you are feeling more like your former, self-assured self. Perhaps the reason you were rejected was that you weren't a good fit or that there were other extenuating circumstances.

You may recognize a mistake you committed and recognize it as a teaching moment. It's also likely that you'll never comprehend all that happened in detail. That's fine too. Whatever happened, you grew and learned from the experience. Because you now understand the procedure, you will be better equipped to identify your feelings the next time you are rejected.

How Does It Feel to Be Rejected?

According to some surprising studies, social rejection actually resembles physical pain in how it feels. Both the sensory and emotional aspects of pain are activated in the corresponding brain areas by this. The pain response increases in intensity with the degree of rejection. Particularly, the brain produced both emotional and physical pain reactions when people thought about a recent romantic relationship breakup. Because of this, when people claim that social rejection hurts, they truly mean it!

Why Being Rejected Stings:

It hurts to be rejected by a friend, a potential romantic partner, or a boss. The misery you experience is real; there's a reason it's called rejection trauma. The same part of your brain is engaged while you're processing this information, whether you're hurting from a finger cut or rejection hurt.

Rejection affects us emotionally as well as physically because we crave acceptance and a sense of belonging. Humans are social beings, and our drive to interact with others has evolved over time. People who quickly assimilated into the tribe were more likely to survive and procreate starting when humans lived together as hunter-gatherer groups.

People who struggled to form strong relationships with others were more likely to be rejected or labeled as outcasts. The demand to be included evolved into a biological requirement over time. The circumstances surrounding rejection conflict with your evolutionary urge, which results in worry and self-doubt.

If you feel these emotions when someone rejects your presence, you are not weak or emotionally unstable. It is biological. You have no control over how you will feel when you are personally disappointed; what you can control is how you will react to the circumstance that is causing these sentiments.

CHAPTER 5
REASONS FOR REJECTION

R ejection is painful. There truly is no getting around that. Most people desire a sense of community and connection, especially with those they care about. No matter if it's for a career, a romantic relationship, or a friendship, it's unpleasant to feel unwelcome and unwanted by those people.

Also, the pain has a rather sharp edge. In reality, rejection causes the same parts of the brain to activate as physical pain does. Hence, it is easy to see why so many individuals fear rejection. If you've passed through rejection once or more, you are likely to remember how painful it was and worry about it occurring again.

However, being afraid of being rejected can prevent you from taking chances and aiming high. Fortunately, with a little effort, it is totally feasible to change this mindset. Here are some pointers to help you get going through rejection. Keep in mind that everyone experiences it. Fear of rejection is a very common emotion, and rejection is a relatively universal experience.

Most people encounter rejection at least a few times in their life for both significant and insignificant reasons, such as:

- A student not receiving an invitation to a friend's party
- A friend ignoring a message about hanging together
- Someone getting rejected for a date
- A long-term partner quitting for another

Some factors behind some of these rejections can be:

- Wrong application or resume
- Inappropriate profile/wrong set of skills
- Not fit
- Physically unfit for any particular employment position
- Passionate but uninterested
- Limited Experience
- Ineffective Communication
- Lack of Confidence
- Insufficient Recommendations
- Excessive Salary Expectations

From the perspective of the candidate, rejection is not a bad thing but rather a practice to learn from and get better for upcoming opportunities. It must be accepted in a healthy way that employment processes include selection and rejection. Even though it never feels nice when things do not go as planned, not all of life's situations pan out as planned. You could feel less afraid of rejection if you remind yourself that it's just a regular part of life and everyone will experience it at some point.

What Brings about Rejection in Relationship?

This is one issue that has remained unresolved for a while. If you have ever experienced rejection in a relationship, you could be left wondering exactly what you did to earn that treatment. Yet, hey! Understanding precisely what leads to rejection in relationships is the first step in preventing this.

- Perhaps your companion isn't ready yet.

One of the main reasons for rejection in relationships is this. Someone who isn't yet prepared for the responsibilities of a relationship with you may struggle and ultimately reject you. If you're the one who's unprepared, the same thing can take place. You can be the one to avoid interacting with your partner.

- Another element that can result in relationship rejection is stress.

When you are with someone who is carrying around a lot of weight at once, they could find it difficult to emotionally connect with you. They may then retreat into their shell as a result, leading you to believe that you have been rejected.

When Do We Experience Rejection?

Although rejection frequently occurs on purpose—that is, when someone rejects you—it doesn't always. The degree to which we are sensitive to rejection and may believe that someone is rejecting us when they are not genuinely differs amongst us. For instance, even if someone isn't trying to reject us, their lack of smile or amusement at our jokes may be taken as rejection.

Women may typically feel rejection more strongly than males. This might be as a result of the fact that women tend to prioritize social ties more than males do. As a result, women may experience rejection in relationships with greater ferocity.

How Do We React When We're Rejected?

Rejection can have some fairly unpleasant effects since it breaks down social relationships and causes us to experience a wide range of negative feelings.

First, it can impair cognitive task performance. All of us have bad ideas and feelings weighing on our minds.

Second, it makes people more aggressive and might possibly result in violence.

Third, it might encourage more self-centered conduct.

Fourth, it can impair our ability to control our impulses—yup, we just ate the entire tub of ice cream because we were feeling rejected!

CHAPTER 6
CONSCIOUSNESS TO REJECTION
How Does Rejection Sensitivity Work?

We vary in how we perceive and respond to rejection, as was already mentioned. While some of us would see our friend's decision not to invite us to lunch as a rejection, others may offer the excuse that they just forgot or didn't anticipate our interest. And the actual intent of our friend can be very different.

Rejection-sensitive people are people who tend to notice when they are rejected in even the tiniest ways—or even believe that they are being rejected when they are not. Therefore, the tendency to "anxiously expect, readily perceive, and overreact to rejection" is classified as rejection sensitivity.

Where Does Sensitivity to Rejection Emanate from?

Many scholars contend that repeated rejections as children, frequently from a parent figure, lead to the development of rejection sensitivity. If our parents or other adults treated us harshly, unfavorably, or negatively when we were young, we may grow to expect the same treatment in interpersonal connections in the present and the future. We could acquire fears of abandonment, shame, and betrayal that cause us to see rejection where it doesn't exist or to notice it when others would not.

What Are the Effects of Rejection Sensitivity on Relationships?

Being rejected might make you more sensitive to rejection, which is a perfectly normal and logical reaction. But just because something makes sense doesn't mean it's good for you. In fact, rejection sensitivity may unintentionally stimulate the rejection-related experiences we seek to avoid.

It might make us feel constantly insecure in our relationships and make us overreact when we feel our partner has rejected us. Relationships can be tested by our aggressive, envious, or dominating behavior brought on by our sentiments of rejection. This is just one example of how altering how we perceive rejection and how we react to it may help us form healthy relationships.

What Does Rejection Sensitivity Dysphoria Mean?

An extreme form of rejection sensitivity called rejection sensitive dysphoria can occasionally be seen in people with autism or attention deficit disorder. These people may have trouble focusing their attention and controlling their emotions. It may be harder to maintain positive reactions to actual or hypothetical rejection as a result.

Fear of Being Rejected

The sensation of rejection is thought to have evolved as a survival mechanism to warn early people who might lose their place in their community. A person was likely to change any harmful conduct after experiencing painful rejection from other tribe members in order to prevent further rejection or ostracism from the group. The likelihood of survival was higher for those who were able to prevent more rejection, whereas the likelihood of survival was lower for those who did not find rejection to be particularly painful and may not have changed the problematic behavior. In this way, it's possible that humans have evolved to find rejection painful.

These days, a lot of people isolate themselves or avoid making connections with others out of a fear of being turned away. Chronic emotions of loneliness and sadness can result from a person withdrawing from others out of fear of or sensitivity to rejection. It is not a recognized diagnosis, despite the fact that rejection sensitivity can co-occur with a variety of mental health conditions, such as social anxiety, avoidant personality, and borderline personality.

Many people with attention-deficit hyperactivity disorder (ADHD) experience rejection sensitivity frequently. Some people with ADHD may have rejection sensitivity dysphoria because they fear rejection so frequently. Self-criticism, social anxiety, and severe melancholy following a perceived rejection are some of the prevalent symptoms of rejection sensitive dysphoria in people with ADHD.

CHAPTER 7
PERSONALITY IMPACTS OF REJECTION
What Has Being Rejected Done to A Person?

People who experience rejection may come to believe that they are not wanted, respected, or accepted, which can be incredibly hurtful. Most people will encounter rejection at least once in their lives. A stressed-out parent may make a child feel rejected momentarily, while a stern or nasty professor may make a student feel rejected.

When someone rejects you, their initial reaction is emotional misery. While some types of rejection can be resolved quickly, such as being rejected by impolite strangers, other types of rejection might have more severe repercussions. Continuous or prolonged rejection can have profound and enduring psychological impacts, which can include:

Trauma: Rejection that lasts for a long time or that causes intense sensations can cause trauma and have negative psychological effects. Children who feel regularly rejected by their parents, for instance, may struggle academically and socially with their classmates. Some people endure a persistent dread of rejection, frequently as a result of several traumatic rejection experiences throughout infancy.

Long-term rejection and extreme rejection can both have a substantial psychological impact on a person. For instance, a child who experiences repeated emotional rejection from their parents may struggle in school or have trouble building relationships later in life because they are afraid of rejection.

Depression: Teenage girls who endure rejection are more likely to develop depression; nevertheless, individuals who encounter rejection may also experience despair. Bullying, which is simply a mix of exclusion and rejection, can also have a variety of detrimental impacts, such as depression, stress, eating disorders, and self-harming behaviors.

There are cases where rejection and depression are related. Even if this only occurs in the most extreme circumstances, the mere chance that rejection can result in depression necessitates dealing with the emotional effects of rejection.

Response to Pain: It has been discovered through research that the brain reacts to social pain in a manner that is comparable to how it reacts to physical pain. Researchers have discovered that social pain, or rejection, activates the same brain pathways as physical pain does. When someone suffers social pain, similar to when physical pain is experienced, receptor systems in the brain also release natural painkillers (opioids).

Rejection can result in bodily agony for a person, while psychological and emotional suffering is more frequently the effects. When you endure physical pain, the same areas of your brain that are activated when you endure emotional anguish are also active.

Stress and Anxiety: Rejection may exacerbate pre-existing symptoms like stress and anxiety or cause their onset. Similar to how these and other mental health issues can heighten rejection feelings.

Rejection can exacerbate the feelings of stress and anxiety if you already struggle with those issues. Being rejected can also lead to anxiety and stress, therefore it's important to pay attention to this.

Abuse: According to a study, male participants' involvement in abusive interpersonal relationships was more common when they had previously experienced higher degrees of parental rejection. Posttraumatic stress disorder symptoms and deficiencies in the processing of social information have also been connected.

Although rejection might be painful, it's never a good idea to use physical or mental abuse or violence against another person to vent your frustration. For instance, a study discovered that feeling rejected might encourage violence or anger toward that group. People who experience rejection can learn to deal with perceived or actual rejection and develop social skills that may enable them to interact with others more readily with the aid of a sympathetic therapist.

Why Does Rejection Hurt So Much?

Being purposefully pushed away from someone you care about is what is meant by rejection. Whether it's a partner, a member of your family, a coworker, or a friend, rejection can still leave you feeling hurt and distressed.

In some relationships, long periods of emotional manipulation may be logically followed by emotional rejection. However, not everyone will be honest about their reasons for rejecting you, and it's typical for you to be unaware of the underlying issue.

This is why rejection can be quite difficult, especially if you are given no justification. Other times, the intensity of the broken connection makes the anguish worse. No matter what kind of rejection you're dealing with, there's a good chance it will leave you feeling upset, have a negative impact on your self-esteem, and in some situations, even make you depressed.

CHAPTER 8
15 RED FLAGS OF REJECTION IN RELATIONSHIPS

Do you feel as though you are being ignored? Here are 15 indicators of rejection in romantic relationships.

1. They never return your calls or texts.

Can you recall how things used to be when your relationship was just getting started? They always returned your calls and texts within a few seconds, giving the impression that they always had their phones with them.

But one of the telltale indications of rejection in a relationship is abrupt silence. They now see your texts but never reply. They never pick up your calls and never call you back.

2. They have drifted apart

It occasionally feels as though you are with a stranger even when you are in the same room as them.

Just now, strategic communication was rendered obsolete. Even though you used to be close friends, you barely talk to one another anymore and love each other's company.

3. You seem to be battling nonstop right now.

You suddenly feel as though you are unable to share the same viewpoint once more. However, the reason you can't seem to stop fighting is generally because they seem to be going out of their way to criticize everything you do.

Now that their expectations have skyrocketed, it seems impossible to please them because there is no chance that they will make any concessions for you.

4. They're constantly busy.

While each relationship partner should have their own life, the importance of spending time together as a pair cannot be overstated. Spending quality time with your partner enhances the quality of your relationship, according to research. But how can this occur when you're with a partner who becomes unexpectedly extremely busy?

When you need them, they never come through. They start working odd hours and traveling far from home all of a sudden. These are a few of the most obvious indications of rejection in a relationship.

5. They claimed they weren't prepared for commitment.

The first time you hear this, you may find yourself rolling your eyes (in the vain hope that they'll get over it quickly). However, if they have a tendency to shove something in your face, you might want to pay more attention.

Even if they say it with a large sneer on their face, a supposed partner who keeps insisting they aren't ready for a commitment is usually trying to avoid your attention and your offers of commitment.

6. They won't give your relationship a name.

Have you ever encountered someone who wants all the advantages couples are entitled to but is never willing to really commit? They long for the affection and closeness that come with being treated like a significant other, but they are never ready to go all the way in.

When you ask them to describe your connection, they shift the subject and refuse to acknowledge that you are nothing more than "friends" with them. It becomes difficult the more you press them to take action.

7. They begin to re-list themselves on the market

When a man (or woman, for that matter) rejects you, one of the most obvious symptoms is that they start to put themselves back out there. When they first met you, they deactivated their dating site accounts. But don't be surprised if you find that they've revived some of those dating sites and are now active there once again. Your partner may be ready to end the relationship if they suddenly start showing interest in dating other people.

8. They start flirting a lot.

It is one thing to have a spouse who acts flirtatious a little bit after drinking too much at a party. However, you might want to reevaluate your relationship if your partner consistently fancies any other eligible individual they come across without regard for your feelings.

You might come across certain folks in your life who really adore the concept of flirting. Even if they are in serious relationships, they may still flirt on occasion. But if they respect and love their relationships, they will restrain themselves from doing this.

However, if your partner continues to flirt with everyone they can, regardless of how you feel, it may be a sign that they are preparing to end the relationship.

9. They've told you from a trusted source.

All the warning indicators we have covered so far are simple to ignore. However, that a close friend or family member of your spouse might soon contribute is one of the most telling signals of rejection in a relationship. This may be the result of anything your partner said to them earlier. Even though you shouldn't see this as the final sign, be careful not to ignore it either.

10. They don't come up with any substantial plans with you.

When someone includes you in their future plans, it is one of the easiest ways to tell if they value you and want to go serious. They talk to you about all the goals they have for the future and express a desire for you to be a part of it.

On the other hand, if your spouse doesn't make any firm arrangements with you, it's a sign that you can start to feel rejected in the relationship shortly. On the other hand, if you are always their fallback and never their top priority, that's a warning flag for you.

11. You haven't yet gotten to know their closest relatives and acquaintances.

If your partner is reluctant to let you meet their family and closest friends, this is one sign that a letdown could be on the horizon. Meeting their family is typically regarded as a significant step toward commitment. However, if you are dating someone who always finds a justification to prevent you from meeting their loved ones, you might want to pause.

Nevertheless, take attention to what they have to say. Has this meeting ever been mentioned? No? Those might be indications of relationship rejection.

12. When you try to introduce them to your family, they withdraw.

Every romantic relationship is influenced by family dynamics, and if your family isn't supportive, your relationship may suffer. It is one thing for your partner to prevent you from seeing their family and friends. However, you might want to reconsider if they consistently withdraw when you try to introduce them to those who are closest to you.

How do they respond when you mention the meeting and introducing your family? When you invite them to meet your closest friends, do they hesitate? This can be the case since they want to pass on you in the future.

13. Suddenly, your sexual life is over.

Your previous sexual life was fantastic. With them, physical closeness was explosive because you two shared a strong emotional bond. At that time, it was difficult to keep your hands separate from one another, and you eagerly anticipated your passionate encounters. Something appears to have gone wrong at the moment.

The couple's sexual life dying naturally is one of the telltale indications of rejection in a relationship. Most of the time, this drop-in sexual activity cannot be linked to a specific cause, such as a health problem, growing responsibility caused by having children, or stress.

Most often, the couple's weakening emotional bond is what causes this drop-in sexual activity. However, if you approach them about having sex, you can even get the cold shoulder.

14. They continue to push you away

Your lover may start abruptly pushing you away as one indication that they are suffering from rejection anxiety. When you try to connect with them (like you once did), they will reject you. When you try to confide in them, they can get hostile and leave. When you try to start a polite conversation with them, they can also try to hurt you verbally.

Pushing you away is one indication that your partner is likely preparing to reject you. When you try to reach out to them for an explanation, though, they won't have any compelling justification for their behavior.

15.You can't rely on them for support any longer

Earlier, you could call them whenever you wanted something. They always delivered on their promise to help you, as you knew they would. But today, the narrative has changed. You find that they are no longer the partner you once knew when you try to reach out to them for solace and a solution. You can reach a point where you no longer turn to them for support or consolation over time.

Rest assured that something may have gone wrong if you can no longer rely on your partner for physical or emotional support.

CHAPTER 9
DEALING WITH REJECTION

Life is about pursuing goals. And when we do, there is always a chance of being rejected. Rejection Has an Impact on Us, Big or Small. All

Rejection need not involve major setbacks like being rejected from your top college choice, failing to make the squad, or not receiving a prom invitation. Feelings of rejection can also result from ordinary events, such as when your joke wasn't received well, no one thought to save you a seat at the lunch table, or when the person you're really into chats to everyone but you.

Whether or not we are rejection sensitive, we may always benefit from learning healthier methods to handle our rejection. This might lessen the physical and emotional suffering that comes with rejection. These techniques can be applied to deal with social rejection from friends or family, rejection in love relationships, and rejection at work. The opposite of feeling accepted is feeling rejected. But being rejected doesn't imply that someone isn't liked, appreciated, or valuable (and we will all experience rejection at times). It just implies that once, in one circumstance, with one individual, things didn't turn out as planned.

Being rejected hurts. But avoiding it totally is impossible. In actuality, you don't want to: People who grow overly terrified of rejection may hesitate to pursue their desires. They may not experience rejection, but they are absolutely certain to pass up the opportunities they don't pursue.

Strategies for Handling Rejection

Here are some strategies for handling rejection:

1. Accept that rejection is an inevitable part of life

Not everything works out as planned. Additionally, rejection can result in progress. It indicates that you're going beyond your comfort zone and taking chances. You're doing something wrong if your life is devoid of rejection.

2. Express your disappointment in writing.

Writing about your emotions and any potential repercussions after receiving rejection may help you process your sentiments more quickly and move past them, according to research. Check out these articles on daily journaling and journaling ideas if you need more advice on writing therapeutically.

3. Develop the ability to accept rejection.

Accepting rejection (rather than analyzing or describing it) could make the unpleasant emotional reactions go away faster. Acceptance does not always come naturally, of course. Remembering that acceptance is different from resignation might be beneficial while practicing acceptance. Tolerating a negative situation or acting like a "doormat" are not examples of acceptance. Simply said, acceptance entails recognizing and accepting who you are, your thoughts, and your feelings. Afterward, you can take necessary action from a position of acceptance.

Denying rejection is the worst reaction to it. It will be more difficult to get over the hurt and disappointment the longer you fool yourself into thinking it doesn't matter. You've been disappointed. Recognize it, along with all the other emotions that accompany the hurt of rejection.

4. Manage your feelings

Make an effort to comprehend your feelings and effectively manage them. Avoid getting angry and venting your frustration on the other person. Rejection does hurt, but that doesn't give you license to hurt other people.

5. Be compassionate with yourself

When facing rejection, it's acceptable to retreat for a while. You need time to take care of yourself and get back on an even emotional keel. Don't criticize or second-guess yourself. Be kind and trust that you'll learn new things when you're ready.

6. Pay attention to the good

Although rejection can be incredibly painful, some research indicates that it may actually make it easier to access happy emotions. This may imply that at this time, positive emotion-based emotion management techniques may be more successful.

7. Keep fit

Keep an eye on your physical and emotional wellness. It's simple to become bogged down in dissatisfaction to the point where you let things slide. Your mind is focused and you are prevented from dwelling on rejection by exercising or learning a new skill. Instead of wallowing in the past, you concentrate on the present.

Getting help from a specialist is necessary if your depressed state persists for more than two weeks despite your best efforts. Contacting a mental health professional is nothing to be afraid of. You can learn coping mechanisms and techniques from a counselor or psychotherapist to help you move on from unfavorable thoughts and feelings of rejection without looking back.

8. Don't let rejection define who you are

It makes sense that your initial response to rejection may be to ask what's wrong with you. When social rejection occurs, a shy person may react by becoming even more of an introvert.

Though you might be the sweetest fruit on the tree, keep in mind that not everyone like peaches. Continue being true to yourself, and you'll draw people who value everything you have to offer.

9. Learn from the encounter

Although rejection hurts, obsessing on your mistakes won't help you move past them. Make an effort to view the situation objectively. Can you draw any conclusions from this? If you were rejected for a job opportunity, ask for constructive criticism to help you figure out how to improve your CV.

Were there any warning signs in the relationship that didn't work out that you ignored along the way? Make use of that knowledge as a foundation to help you get ready the next time you decide to put yourself out there.

10. Consider removing yourself emotionally from the rejection.

Imagine being a fly on the wall or a stranger on the street as you experience rejection when you emotionally distance yourself. The unpleasant emotions may go more rapidly if you consider your circumstance from the viewpoint of someone else.

11. Use acetaminophen to lessen rejection pain

A really intriguing study revealed that taking Tylenol (acetaminophen) after being rejected actually reduced the wounded sentiments. Therefore, a Tylenol may be helpful if you're feeling desperate to lessen the sting of rejection. However, you can do without it as it may have side effects.

12. Recognize your emotions.

It hurts notwithstanding where the rejection came from. Even while other people might think it's not a big problem and tell you to go on, the sorrow might linger, especially if you happen to be more sensitive to rejection. Other uneasy feelings, such awkwardness and embarrassment, might accompany rejection. Only you have the ability to express your feelings to others. It's crucial to accept your sentiments of rejection before you can start to deal with them. If you lie to yourself and say you don't care if you are wounded when in reality you do, you lose the chance to face and effectively deal with this fear.

13. Seek out the educational opportunities

Even while it may not appear that way at first, rejection can present chances for personal growth.

Imagine that you apply for a job that you really want and that you had a fantastic interview, but you are not hired. You could initially be devastated by this. Nevertheless, after giving your résumé another check, you would realize it wouldn't hurt to review some of your skills and pick up some new software usage.

After a few months, you would realize that the new information has given you access to higher-paying jobs for which you were before unqualified. It can be simpler to go after what you want and less painful if you fail if you reframe your anxiety as an opportunity for progress. If something doesn't work out, try reminding yourself, "This may not work out, but if it doesn't, I'll have a meaningful experience and know more than I did."

Reviewing what you actually want in a mate will help you overcome rejection anxieties when it comes to romantic relationships. It may also make you to be on the right track to locating a match right away.

14. Convince yourself of your value

When you take rejection too personally, it can be truly frightening. For instance, you might be concerned that you bored a date partner or that they didn't find you attractive enough if they abruptly quit responding to your texts after a few dates.

However, needs mismatching is frequently the cause of rejection.

Ghosting is never a good strategy, but some individuals simply don't know how to communicate well or believe that being honest by expressing, "You're nice and cute, but I didn't quite feel it," will make you feel upset when, in reality, you'll enjoy it.

You may recall that you are completely deserving of love by increasing your self-worth and confidence, which will make you feel less hesitant to continue looking for it.

Try:

- identifying five ways you live out your personal principles;
- writing a paragraph describing three instances when you are most pleased of yourself;
- and reminding yourself of the benefits you can bring to a relationship.
15. Maintain your sense of perspective

You might imagine numerous worst-case scenarios if you are more sensitive to rejection and spend a lot of time worrying about it. Let's say you weren't accepted into the graduate program of your choice. You may begin to worry that you will be rejected by every program you applied to and will have to try again the following year.

But then you start to fear that you'll be turned down again the following year, which will make it impossible for you to land the job you want and advance your career, which will make it impossible for you to ever become financially stable enough to realize your dream of home ownership and starting a family, and so on.

Catastrophizing is a form of negative mental loop that is typically unfounded. Create a few actionable backup plans for yourself or come up with arguments to dispel some of your biggest concerns.

16. Identify what rejection actually frightens you.

You can deal with that specific anxiety by investigating what's really driving your fear of rejection. Perhaps you are worried about being rejected romantically because you don't want to be alone. Realizing this can also encourage you to prioritize making lasting friendships, which can protect you from loneliness. Or perhaps you are concerned about getting turned down by possible employment because you lack a backup plan and feel insecure about your financial situation. If you don't immediately land the job you're looking for, outlining a few potential techniques may be helpful.

17. Confront your phobia

It's true that you won't face rejection if you don't put yourself out there. But you'll also probably fail to meet your objectives. You have a chance to succeed if you go after what you desire. It's possible that you'll be rejected, but it's also possible that you won't.

A "fear hierarchy," or a list of steps connected to your fear of rejection, can be created. Each step can then be tackled one at a time. Exposure treatment includes this. While you can try this on your own, a therapist can also assist you in making a list and working through it.

Someone who is terrified of being rejected romantically may start by making a dating profile without any plans to use it right away. After then, they can start corresponding without any plans to meet in person. Just be sure to let folks know that you aren't yet looking to meet if you choose to do this.

18.   Reject self-defeating thoughts

After receiving rejection, it's simple to develop a habit of self-criticism. It's possible for you to utter phrases like "I knew I'd mess that up," "I didn't prepare enough," "I talked too much," or "I'm so boring."

Nevertheless, this only serves to confirm your perception that you were to be blamed for the rejection, even when it might not have been your fault at all. A self-fulfilling prophecy can emanate if you think someone will reject you because you aren't good enough, which can force you to act in fear.

Although it doesn't always work that way, positive thinking may help you see things in a clearer way. You're more likely to believe in your ability to achieve your goals when you support and encourage yourself. If things don't work out, try to be compassionate with yourself by telling yourself what you would tell a loved one in a similar circumstance.

19. Rely on your network of supporters

It can help you to feel more wanted if you spend time with individuals who care about you. A strong support system provides consolation if your efforts fail and encouragement when you try to accomplish your goals. The prospect of rejection may look less terrifying when you know that your loved ones will support you no matter what happens. You can also practice exposing yourself to rejection situations with trusted pals if you're nervous about it.

20.   Consult a specialist

Fear of rejection may have long-lasting impacts, such as keeping you from pursuing significant possibilities at your place of work or school. Even if you can surmount your anxieties of rejection on your own, getting professional assistance can occasionally be very helpful. If your fear of rejection:

- causes you to experience anxiety or panic attacks, it might be time to think about seeing a therapist.
- prevents you from doing things you wish to do
- upsets your regular life

What to Do

Less rejection hurts us as we become more adept at handling it. How can you then develop that capacity for adjustment?

These are some concepts:

- Be truthful.
- Utilizing both your thoughts and feelings are key components of effective rejection coping.

Starting with emotions, tell yourself whether you've been rejected. Do not attempt to downplay your suffering or act as if it is not there. Consider how distinct it is to feel the way you do, given your circumstances, rather than feeling like "I shouldn't feel this way." Take note of how strong your emotions are. Did this rejection really make you angry? Or only a little bit? You can cry if you want to; crying is a healthy method to get emotions out.

Next, describe how you are feeling. As an illustration: "I'm very sad that I wasn't selected for the school play. I have worked so hard and wanted it so badly. Because my friends succeeded and I did not, I feel excluded. Tell someone else what occurred and how you feel about it if you want to. Choose a supportive and receptive person.

For two reasons, telling someone else can be beneficial and they are:

- Knowing that someone empathizes with your situation and how you feel can be comforting.
- You are compelled to express your emotions verbally.

Acknowledging feelings can help you get through difficult emotions, whether you want to talk about them with someone else or keep them to yourself.

- Be Upbeat

It's very easy to become consumed by a negative emotion like rejection when you're going through it. But concentrating on the bad things can make it feel like you're reliving the experience. In addition to continuing to get hurt, it gets more difficult to overcome the rejection.

Accept your feelings, but try not to let them consume you. Keep it out of your constant conversation and thought. Why? Our behaviors and expectations are influenced by negative thinking. Rejection could even increase if you stay entrenched in a negative frame of mind. It undoubtedly discourages someone from giving it another shot.

Track Listing for Examining Your Thought

Let's hear your opinion now: Take into account your justifications for being rejected. Do you put yourself down too much? It is generally normal to ask why did it happen. You should reserve your justifications to the facts when you give yourself an explanation.

Justify your actions by saying that you got turned down for prom because the person didn't want to go with you. Don't tell yourself things like "I'm such a loser" or "I got rejected because I'm not attractive." None of these are true. They are overanalyzing the event and imagining a motive. Shut off any derogatory thoughts that may start to enter your head.

Self-blame or self-deprecating thoughts can accentuate our flaws and cause us to believe things about ourselves that are just plain untrue. This way of thinking stifles hopes and self-confidence, which are just what we need to move past feeling lousy and desire to try again.

If you start putting yourself down or blaming yourself for the rejection, you can start to think you'll always be rejected. Illusions like "I'll never get a date" or "No one will ever like me" magnify a simple rejection to the point of catastrophe. Even while rejection might be extremely painful and demoralizing, it's not the end of the world.

Maintaining Perspective

"Yeah, I got rejected this time," tell yourself. Maybe I'll get a "yes" when next I have the opportunity," or "Oh well. This is what took place. It bothers me. It's not how I had envisioned things to go. However, rejection happens to everyone, so I can try again.

Think on your strengths and positive qualities. Keep in mind the occasions when you received approval, made the cut, or received a "yes." Consider everyone who likes and supports you.

Reward yourself for your efforts. It's fantastic that you took a chance. Remember that you can deal with the rejection. Even though you were rejected right now, there will be another chance later. Get metaphysical Things occasionally occur for reasons that we don't always comprehend.

Make the Most of Rejection

Rejection gives people the time to think about what they can improve. It's acceptable to consider where you can improve or whether your objectives were too lofty. Maybe you need to work on your game, your academics, your interview approach, or whatever it takes to increase your chances of getting accepted the next time if your talents weren't strong enough this time. Make sure you make the most of the chance to get better by using the rejection.

Rejection can serve as a hard reality check. Nevertheless, if you go about it the right way, it might be able to point you in the path that ends up being the ideal match for your skills, personality, and all the other splendid qualities that make you who you are.

CHAPTER 10
THE CONSEQUENCES OF REJECTION

So, here's the unpleasant truth: Rejection in a relationship has its traditional warning signs. Some things that your spouse won't ever do to you unless they're attempting to tell you they're no longer interested in the relationship with you. Despite the obviousness of these warning flags, the fear of being abandoned can keep you in a relationship for a long period when you should be going on with your life.

The Consequences of Rejection and How to Get over the Fear of Rejection

Relationship rejection can be quite damaging to the person who received it. For starters, individuals might start experiencing rejection anxiety, which makes them approach any new connection with the fear that they will soon be rejected once more. On the other hand, rejection can have untold negative implications on a person's self-esteem. The person who was rejected can have self-esteem problems for a while if they don't fully recover.

Has someone rejected you? So that you may continue living your life, here's how to get over your fear of rejection.

1. Don't let it get to you

One of the hardest things you'll hear today is certainly this. Nevertheless, it demands to be said. To start overcoming rejection in a relationship, you must first acknowledge that you had nothing to do with it.

2. Give yourself ample time to accept your feelings and recover.

It happens frequently that the first thing you'll do when you grow sick of being rejected in a relationship is to leave and start over. Rebounds, according to research, are more harmful than beneficial. Take all the time you need to heal after ending the toxic relationship. Return to yourself. Get new interests. More buddies to make. Before you enter a new relationship, rediscover who you are and take good care of yourself.

3. A professional may be necessary.

To completely recover from the effects of relationships like these, you can occasionally need professional assistance. Now, consulting a specialist is one method for overcoming the anxiety of being rejected in a romantic relationship. Consider consulting a therapist, psychologist, or mental health professional.

How To Manage the Pain of Rejection

We all seek and require the ability to experience acceptance, love, and caring. It is one of the fundamental psychological requirements for living that begin in childhood and continue all the way to adulthood. Due to this, experiencing emotional neglect of any kind or degree as well as the fear of doing so are harsh and unstable. And why it hurts even when someone you care about ignores you.

If any of these psychological conditions are causing you mental stress right now, you might want to consider enrolling in a love addiction intensive class where you can learn techniques for reducing, accepting, and overcoming rejection pain. The first step in improving your emotional well-being is to get knowledge about the specifics of emotional rejection and how, if ignored, they can have a detrimental effect on your life.

Why Does Rejection Lead to Obsession?

On the one hand, even the dread of being rejected by someone you care about, romantically or in another way, can cause us to develop clingy and compulsive behavioral habits.

On the other side, there is a biological justification for why rejection might result in obsessive behavior. The same areas of our brain that keep us motivated are stimulated by romantic rejection.

Additionally, it influences the areas of our brain that are connected to addiction, rewards, and cravings. This is the physiologic explanation for why you frequently experience sentiments of obsessive attachment after someone rejects you romantically.

There are other methods to account for this compulsive psychological trend, though. For instance, you might believe it's your fault and be making amends for your errors. Maybe you still believe that person to be your ideal match. Regardless of the causes, rejection frequently has compulsive effects.

What Is the Best Way to Handle Rejection in A Relationship?

There are healthy, effective ways to deal with emotional rejection. Without the aid of experienced relationship advocates, your efforts to beat love addiction may occasionally fail. This should not, however, discourage you from attempting to use the following methods:

- **Consider Everything**

Give yourself the luxury of allowing all emotions to pass through you, both good and bad. Allow yourself to encounter each one. Avoid running away from them or attempting to push them away. Accept them, and take action to begin your rehabilitation.

- **Recognize The Pain**

Be careful not to go into denial. Be realistic and accept the truth that you will hurt and that things will soon become painful. The beginning of the healing process happens during this phase of comprehension and acceptance.

- **Stop Blaming Yourself**

People who are experiencing rejection frequently begin blaming themselves right away while idealizing the other person. But understand that it wasn't all your fault. It takes two to make a tango, and two to break one.

- **Give Yourself Some Mercy**

Don't just stop at abstaining from self-blame. Take it a step further and be kind to yourself. Be in the company of those who will support and show you care. Do this because you deserve to have friends who will understand you and listen to you without passing judgment, not because you need anyone's approval or acceptance.

- **Keep It from Defining You**

The unpleasant emotions that are currently circling around inside of you do not fully define who you are. You are more than the suffering you're going through and the person who was just turned down. Remember that you are more than how you currently feel.

- **Understand It**

Learn from your experiences as well as your faults, including how you were handled, how your relationships developed, and how they ended. You'll find comfort in the idealistic, rose-colored picture if you spend some time making it more realistic.

- **Never Be Afraid to Ask for Help**

Finally, don't be afraid to ask for assistance. There are qualified relationship advocates who have the experience and understanding to assist those who are experiencing similar issues to you. A wide range of problems, such as rejection, emotional attachment, love addiction and fixation, etc., can be addressed by professionals. They can guide you through it all and help you spot problematic behavioral patterns that you can alter.

How Can You Distinguish Your Self-Worth from Romantic Rejection?

One of the most painful sorts of rejection is romantic rejection. It pierces right through the core of who we are and how appealing we think we are. No one is exempt, either. Rejection is a worry that over 70% of people have, especially when it comes to their age and appearance. This confirms what women have told us.

The pain of a love rejection can last longer if you have low self-esteem or have experienced trauma. Thankfully, most people can overcome the terrible emotions by relying on supportive friends or family. However, those of us who already suffer from low self-esteem and hold repressed memories of childhood trauma may experience delays of months, if not years.

So, how might we lessen our own suffering? We don't get along with everyone we meet, let's face it; if we did, we would be best friends with everyone we have ever met. Dating gives us the chance to discover more about who we are and what we want, as well as to develop our resilience via interactions with both the right people and the wrong ones. Therefore, when someone rejects you, the universe is guiding you toward suitable partners who are deserving of you, your time, and your love in addition to saving you precious time. Therefore, rejection is beneficial since it both teaches us something and pushes us closer to our objectives and pleasure.

No one is rejecting you; the relationship is

Rejection never has a specific target. If our spouse breaks up with us, it's more likely due to a problem with the relationship than it is to do with us specifically, she explains. "Separating our sense of self from the combined self we become when we bond with other people can be really empowering."

We also need to understand that rejection is never entirely personal; it's often reflective of key needs or wants that aren't being met within a mutual dynamic. Therefore, when someone breaks up with you or declines to pursue the relationship further, it's not necessarily you as a person who is being rejected.

CHAPTER 11
ADVANTAGES OF REJECTION

The regrettable but important aspect of the human experience is rejection. Whether or not they are aware of it, everyone encounters rejection at some point in their lives. The advantages of rejection are something that many people who go through this never fully comprehend. This may seem counterintuitive, but just ask anyone who has ever been turned down for a job or had a loved one declare they weren't interested in them that way. If you only look at rejection the proper way, it can actually be a pretty beneficial thing most of the time. Here are 10 advantages of rejection you should take into account the next time you find yourself in this circumstance.

1. Being rejected inspires us to work harder.

Rejection can be an indication that you need to start doing something you're not currently doing or quit doing something you are now doing. You will be on the road to doing better and encountering less rejection in the future once you identify what it is.

2. Rejection teaches us that we are only human.

Each person is the star of their own story, which can cause an understandable but false sense of self-importance in the grand scheme of things. Everyone could need being knocked down a peg or two at some point, therefore rejection is actually a good thing. No matter how amazing we'd like to think we are, rejection serves to remind us that we're all simply human.

3. Rejection helps you develop patience.

Rejection can come in many different forms, some of which are painful while others are downright catastrophic. One of the toughest rejections can be not getting the job you spent a month sending resumes, emails, and faxes back and forth for because the bills and the cupboard don't give a damn about your broken feelings. Rejection, however, might teach you to be patient and keep going in this situation, so take advantage of it. Even though you might not immediately receive what you want, if you're ready to put in the necessary effort and have patience, you will eventually arrive at your desired destination.

4. Rejection inspires us to take alternative routes.

Rejection can occasionally be life's way of letting us know that the best way to achieve our goals is by choosing a different route. The route we're trying to follow may not be the best one for us, or perhaps there is a superior one that we haven't yet discovered. If you're willing to try a different route or find a new approach to accomplish the same goal, rejection can be a great experience.

5. Rejection makes us reassess who we are.

Many people have trouble accepting rejection. That is normal. Rejection hurts and is unpleasant. However, when something is repeated enough times, people usually begin to pay attention. An example of such a rejection is, "You're not too hot at dealing with other people, but you have great skills with numbers." One key benefit of rejection that people frequently overlook is the ability to reinvent oneself by becoming more goal- or people-oriented or by changing aspects of our personalities to get along better with those around us.

6. Rejection causes us to reevaluate our objectives.

The person who struggles through an MBA degree because they've been told their entire lives that it's the key to success and power when what they actually want to do is play the violin in an orchestra is an example of how as species, we often overlook warning signs that are there for our benefit. After the interview, the candidate is informed that they were egregiously underqualified. A third-chair violinist is also needed by the neighborhood orchestra. Your desires will always come through, and sometimes rejection forces us to choose between the "safe goal" that would ultimately leave us unhappy and the impossibly difficult ambition we've always wanted to pursue.

7. Rejection offers chances for improvement.

Consider the last time someone claimed he would never have found a job, met the person or moved to a place if the other place hadn't refused to hire him or a person hadn't refused to marry him or a town had more jobs available. Rejection can be a strong motivator for us to examine why we pursue the goals we do and what it is about them that motivates us to continue toward, or abandon, these ambitions. It can also be an excellent opportunity to reflect on why one pursues particular goals, people, positions, or circumstances. As a race, we would be much happier and more secure in our abilities and instincts if we would just take the time to listen to what these things are telling us about ourselves.

8. Rejection opens our eyes to fresh perspectives.

Everybody occasionally has tunnel vision. We give all of our attention to a single objective, to a person, or to a dream. Rejection can force one to take a step back and reconsider one's goals and methods for achieving them. In this situation, it's important to adopt a fresh perspective and think about alternative approaches to achieving the same end result as well as how we view our own aspirations and ambitions.

9. Rejection makes us more resilient.

There's an adage that the fish that swims upstream is the strongest. Although rejection frequently seems to stop you in your tracks, in actuality it offers you something to push against. People don't become stronger when everything goes their way, but rather when they have to deal with the unexpected or unpleasant. In this regard, rejection is beneficial since it demonstrates our true strength, resiliency, and capacity under pressure.

10. Rejection presents a chance for development.

Rejection does not always have to be a bad thing. Instead, consider viewing rejection as an opportunity for you to develop personally. Perhaps you discover via rejection that your aftershave causes sinus headaches or that your temperament in a professional setting turns people away. Any area of your life can benefit from the lessons you learn through rejection, which will help you become a stronger, nicer, and more "polished" person.

You can envisage that rejection can be terrible, but it can also turn out to be a blessing in disguise. What remains to be seen is how you will respond to rejection. Will you seize the chance it is presenting you with or have the skylight installed in your living room? Your decision is yours.

CHAPTER 12
CONCLUSION

Rejection hurts your emotions in a serious way. Your self-worth and confidence may be damaged. You could need some time to develop your sense of self-love and self-esteem if you're having trouble getting over a setback.

Someone who has a strong sense of self-worth can bounce back from rejection more successfully. Knowing that you are the one who recognizes your qualities means you may move on with assurance. Healthy self-esteem and confidence do not guarantee that you will never experience rejection again. That is not feasible. But when the inevitable occurs, you'll be able to acknowledge, embrace, and process the feelings the experience engenders, comprehend where they come from, and know that no matter the initial unpleasantness, you'll be fine.

Rejection can hurt and make you question your abilities. But if you live in fear of it, you might be restricted and miss out on a lot of what life has to offer. You may experience a reduction in your fear of rejection if you decide to view it as a chance for personal development rather than as something you cannot change.

This pain is no exception to the rule that pain eventually goes away. It could not matter very much in a year or even a few months. A therapist can provide advice if you need help getting over this worry.

Make the Best of It

It's critical to keep in mind that rejection can save you from squandering time in the wrong relationships. Despite the fact that many people fear offending the other person when they want to end an undefined romantic relationship, a large majority of people would like to know if the other person isn't interested in them. This demonstrates how "rejection" is merely how each person wants a mutually thrilling connection and has nothing to do with a person's value. Romantic love is centered on this, after all.

Rejection is a step in the process that brings us closer to our goal. Therefore, in actuality, love rejections are not a reflection of your value but rather are road signs and redirections all set up to help you attain your relationship goals. It is your responsibility to work toward internal happiness and wellbeing. Consider making improving your mental health a top priority if rejection has left you feeling depleted. Making the most of this self-care time will help you achieve your future dating and relationship goals with greater resiliency, energy, and mental clarity. When you find someone who merits you, you can concentrate on finding them.

I would go back in time and convince myself that there was nothing about me that needed to be fixed or altered. Rejection definitely hurts, and the pain may last a little while depending on how we're feeling about ourselves at the time. Take as much time as you need to process your pain, but keep in mind that the rejection really is about them, not you. There is always someone who will accept you for who you are.

Printed in Great Britain
by Amazon

24032166R00046